A

PECULIAR

TREASURE

Emmanuel O. Afolabi

Revival Waves of Glory Books & Publishing
PO Box 596
Litchfield, IL 62056
https://www.revivalwavesofgloryministries.com/

Published in the United States of America

Paperback: 9781980517405

Table of Contents

FOREWARD

I feel honored to write the foreword of this wonderful book written by our beloved Brother Afolabi.

The book enlightens the readers the need for obedience and humility among all other things to be peculiar treasure. Remember, God demands total obedience from us, only then can we fully benefit from God.   (I Samuel 15:22).

God resist the proud but gives grace to the humble James 4:6. Without humility, no one can go far in life. It is therefore necessary for us to be humble. When we obey and are humble, we stand the chances of reaping bountiful reward.

The book, A peculiar Treasure is a must read for every believer and all those who want to have personal encounter with God and wish to receive His numerous blessings.

When you know what it requires of you to be peculiar, then strive hard to attain it. It is very important to note that the Christian journey is all about firm determination.

The book will be useful to help readers become what God wants them to be. The thought of God towards us is of peace and not of evil to give us our expected end. (Jere.29:11).

As you read through this book and apply the principles therein, you will become a peculiar treasure unto God. Shalom.

Rev. (Mrs) F.B. Badejo
Asst. Minister
Foursquare Gospel Church in Nigeria.
Zion Assembly
Ije-Ododo
Lagos Nigeria.

ACKNOWLEDGMENT

Glory is unto God, great things He has done in helping me to accomplish the desire to put up this work.

I sincerely acknowledge the contribution of the Assisting Minister Rev. (Mrs)F.B.Badejo of our Foursquare Gospel Church in Nigeria Zion Assembly who wrote the foreword for his/her interest in seeing that the project is a huge success, my beloved Deacon Wale Ogunleye who wrote about the book. He indeed increased my enthusiasm, bolstered my moral and motivated me to work harder. Thanks go to my daughter Margret Ore-Oluwa Afolabi who created most of her valuable time to edit the book.

I also appreciated the contribution of few friends who showed interest in this work. It is my prayer that the Lord will reward them all in abundance.

DEDICATION

I dedicate this book to all my dear readers that as you read through the pages of this book, the Lord will show-forth Himself strongly to you, and open your eyes of understanding to comprehend the purpose of His calling for your life and grant you His enabling grace to be obedient to his directives that will lunch you into His everlasting covenant of those who trust and obey Him.

As you aspire to be a peculiar treasure unto the Lord. Walk in obedience. Shalom.

Emmanuel O. Afolabi

PROLOGUE

"The Holy Bible (NKJV). The Bible contains the mind of God, the state of man, the way of salvation, the doom of sinners, and happiness of believers, its doctrines are holy, its precepts are bindings, its holiness are true and its decisions are immutable. Read it to be wise, believe it to be safe, and practice it to be holy. It contains light to direct you, food to support you, and comfort to cheer you.

It is the traveler'smap, the pilgrim's staff, the pilot's compass, the soldier's sword, and the Christians'charter. Here paradise is restored, heaven opened, and the gate of hell disclosed.

CHRIST is its grand subject and the glory of God its end. It should fill the memory, rule the heart, and guide the feet. Read it slowly, frequently and prayerfully. It is mine of wealth a paradise of glory, and a river of pleasure. It is given for life, will be opened forever. It involves the highest responsibility.

Will reward as greatestlabor and will condemn all who triple with thesacred contents? Extracts from Gideon Pocket Bible, the Holy Bible (NKJV &KJV) Oxford Advanced Learner's Dictionary (6th Edition) and English Mini Dictionary (New Edition).

INTRODUCTION

The English Mini Dictionary (New Edition) defined peculiar as belonging to a person and to him only, while treasure things such as gold, silver, jewels etc. You are God treasure, as Christ taught us "For where your treasure is there will your heart be also (Luke 12:34) We're therefore a special possession which is over and above all else, a purchased, acquisition of high value who is sealed up (Eph.4:30) preserved and saved unto the time appointed of God's purpose when we shall show-forth the glory and perfection of sonship from Him who has called us out of darkness into the marvelous light (I Peter 2:9)l What a different we are in comparison to a mere metal treasure of this world that perish way.

Regardless what people see or say, it should not concern the peculiar people. I have not come across Christian who believes they are not a part of elect entity. Everyone embraces this verse and hold it as their own. They all believe and say that they are members of this chosen generation, the royal priesthood. They maintain that they are Holy Nation and especially a peculiar people indeed.

But this claim goes beyond affirmative, because the pre-requisite to attested to the claim is that there must be a personal encounter with Christ and the born-again spirit must dwell within to present one to the Father as Peculiar Treasure (John 1:12). Furthermore the saying of Apostle Peter buttress this point "They stumbled at the word and astone of stumbling and a rock of offence, even to them which stumble at the word, being disobedience where unto also they were appointed" (I Peter2:8).Means not obeying God's voice nor keeping His Covenant is direct opposite to His demand. "Now therefore, if you will obey my voice indeed and keep my covenant then you shall be a peculiar treasure unto me" (Exodus 19:.5)

God is God of principles. He will not bend is rules to accommodate us, hence the attached condition to this covenant blessing is not negotiable. You must adhere strictly by hearken to His voice and keep the covenant, in doing so, it will provide way for you to enter into the family of God, because you have been made perfect in Christ Jesus before the foundation of the world was laid, by Him all things consist.

"And He is before all things and by Him allthing consist".(Col. 1:17)NKJV

As we voyage to the land of Treasure, let us adhere strictly to rules and regulations of listening and hearken in obedience, so that the will of our God may prevail in our walking with Him. Shalom.

Emmanuel O. Afolabi

CHAPTER ONE

WHAT DOES THE LORD REQUIRED OF YOU

Micah 6:8 says "He has shown you 'O man what is good; and what does the Lord require of you, but to do justly and to love mercy, and to walk humbly with your God".

To refresh our mind, we shall examine this requirements one after the others:

1. **To do Justly**: - it mean to love our neighbor and ourselves and to give that what is due to them, not what is due in our own eyes, but what is due in God's eyes. Can we sin against a loved one, perhaps we might momentarily sin against a loved one, but not continually. However we are not togive that which is due to God to any man, neighbor or self. Therefore it beholds on us as creation of God to love Him with our totality and our affectionate must be unparalleled, because He formed us in our mother's womb and at the time appointed, He separate us and brought us forth. Also be reminded that this is the first commandment to love God with all our hearts, souls and strength. In addition to

give to yourself what is due, according to saying of Apostle Paul we are not our own, we are purchase with priceless treasure, hence our bodies are the temple of the Holy Spirit (I Corinth:6:19) so the need to adherent strictly to the Paul's advice in (Gal:5:19-25) is paramount of what we must flee away from and what we must embrace.

2. **To Love Mercy:-** God realized what man has come to know Justice while it is necessary, but at times we are cool and unfeeling toward others. To be justly alone is not sufficient for a child of God; it's must graduate to love mercy and what it requires. Mercy comes from characteristics that include, kindness, benevolent and charity. Part of what mercy require is to be willing to forgive those that sin against us. It is this aspect of mercy through which our own salvation comes.

"Not by works of righteousness which we have done, but according to his mercy he saved us by the washing orregeneration and renewing of the Holy Ghost". Titus 3-5

3. **To Walk In Humility**: To walkhumbly. But how are we to do this? We must first andforemost acknowledged oursins and then be willing tosubmit to God's mercy. It

isonly through a humbling ofourselves that we be allowedto walk with God. "God resist the proud, but give grace to the humble".(I Peter 5:5) what then is good? God requires is thedoings of His will; submitting to God through obedience to His desire and directives, thenhis grace will multipleupon us.

"Humble yourself thereforeunder the mighty hand ofGod, that he may exalt you in due time".I Peter 5:6.KJV.

The perfect example of humility and mercy is that of David who spares Saul's life in I Samuel 21. Now it happened when Saul had returned from following the Philistines, that it was told that David is in the wilderness of EnGed; then Saul took three thousand chosen men from all Israel and went to seek David and his men on the rocks of the Wild Goats. Without knowing to Saul he comes to a cave where David and his men are hiding. So he came to the sheepfolds by the road, where was a cave and Saul went in to attend to his needs. David and his men were staying in the recesses of the cave. This was not coincidence,but arranged by God to test David and to train him and to also display the godly heart of David.

Then the men of Davidsaid to him. This is the day of which the LORD said to you! Behold I will deliver your enemy into your hand that you may do to him as it seems good to you. David arose and secretly cut off acorner of Saul's robe. Now it happened afterward that David's heart trouble him said to his men. "The LORD forbids that I should to this thing to mymaster, the Lord's anointed, to stretch out my hand against him. Seeing he is the anointed of the LORD. So David restrained his servants with these words, and did not allow them to rise against Saul.

David's men were excited at the opportunity at their disposal, believed it was all a gift from God. They knew it was no coincidence that Saul comes aloneinto the cave at that moment. So, they thoughtthis was an opportunity to kill Saul. Why are they excited? Their lives as fugitives are about to end, they will soon be installed as friends and associates of the new king in Israel.

But David refused to kill Saul, because he know that God's promise said "You will inherit the throne of Israel. He actually know that Saul was in the way of that promise, he also realized that it will be disobedient if he kill Saul, because at that time God put Saul in aposition of authority *and it was God's business to take care of Saul, not David,he wantedthe promise to be fulfilled, hencehe refused to try and fulfill God's promise through his own disobedience.*

"Let every soul be subject untothe higher powers for there isno power, but of God, the powerthat be are ordained of God". Roman 13:1

Dear readers! Sometimes when we have a promise from God we must be careful not too justified in sinning to pursue that promise.This is always wrong. Don't take advantage when it comes to the promise of God for your life, because you may end up with a great consequences.

Many people in David's situation would find many excuses to justify killing Saul it was self-defense, because Saul was out to kill me, it's all right, because God promised me the throne anyway, it's all right because I'm in the right and even Jonathan knows thatI deserved the throne. This is a God given opportunity and I should take it, or even, I'm just so tired of running and fight Saul. This can end all of that now. But David refused to make any such excuses and had a radical obedient trust in God instead. David couldn't have read the book of Romans yet, but he knew its truth better than most who have. "Don't be overcome by evil, but overcome evil with good" (Romans 12:21).

In all this, we see that David knew not only to wait on the Lord, but he also knew how to wait for the LORD: we wait on the Lord by prayer and supplication, looking for the indication of His will. We wait for the Lord by patience and submission looking for the inter position at his hand.

David was determined that when he sat on the throne of Israel, it wouldn't be because he got Saul out of the way, but because God got Saul out of the way. He wanted God's fingerprint in that work, not his own, and he wanted the clean conscience that come from knowing it was God's work.

We also see that David's heart didn't store up bitterness and anger towards Saul even as Saul made David's life completely miserable. David kept talking it to the Lord and he received the cleansing from the hurt and the bitterness, and the anger that the Lord can give. If David had stored up bitterness and anger towards Saul, he probably wouldn't have been able to resist the temptation to kill him at what seemed to be a "risk free" opportunity.

We win most when we appear to have yielded most, and gain advantages by refusing to take them wrongfully. The man who can wait for God's promise, is a man of power, what a tender conscience of David! Many would only be troubled that they did not take the opportunity to kill Saul. David only cut off the corner of Saul's robe. Yet his heart troubled him why? Because the robewas a symbol of Saul's royal authority and David felt bad, rightly so, according to the heart of God, that he had done anything against Saul's God appointed authority. This is David expression when he said "The Lord forbids that I should do this thing to my master the LORD's anointed..... Seeing he is the anointed of the LORD".

So David restrained his servants with this words. What words? The word of a humble, tender conscience before God. The words of a man who was convinced at merely cutting off a corner of Saul's robe. When David's servant saw how godly David was, and how much he wanted to please God in everything their heart were restrained from doing any evil against Saul.

Then David also arose afterward, went out of the cave, follow afterSaul and called to Saul, saying My Lord the King, when Saul looked behind him, David stopped with his face on the earth, and bowed down, David took a big change here, because he could have simply remained in hiding, secure in the fact that Saul had not found him. Buthe surrendered himself to Saul, because he saw the opportunity to prove his innocence and to show his heart towards him, he also showed great trust in God, because he made himself completely Vulnerable to Saul. Saul could killed him very easily at that moment, but David trusted that if he did what was right before God, God would protect him and fulfill the promise.

Then David said to Saul, why do you listen to the word of men, who say. Indeed David seek your harm? look this day your eyes have seen that the LORD delivered you today into my hand in the cave, and someone urged me to kill you. But my eye spares you. I said I will not stretch out my hand against my Lord, for he is the Lord's anointed .However, My Father, see! Yes see the corner of your robe in my hand! for in that I cut off the corner of your robe, and did not kill you. Know and see that there is neither evil nor rebellion in my hand, and I have not sinned against you. Yet you hurt my life to take it, let the LORD judge between you and me, and let the LORD avenge me and you. But my hand shall *notbe against you. As the proverbs of the ancients says wickedness proceeds from the wicked. but my hand not be against you. After whom has the king of Israel come out? Whom do you pursue? A dead dog? A flea?*

Therefore let the Lord be judge and judge between you and me, and see and plead my case, and deliver me out of your hand.

David actually knew the type of man who Saul was, but he prudently and modestly translates the fault from Saul to his followers and evil counselors.

Here is Saul's emotional reaction to David. So it was, when David had finished speaking these words to Saul that Saul said. Is this your voice my Son David? He lifted up his voice and wept. Then he said to David, you are more righteous than I, for you have reward me with good, whereas I have rewarded you with evil, you have shown this day how you have dealtwell with me, for when the LORD delivered me into your hand, you did not kill me. For if a man finds his enemy, will he let him get away safely? Therefore may the Lord reward you with good for what you have done to me this day! Surely you shall be king and that the kingdom of Israel shall be established in your hand. Therefore swear now to me by the LORD that you will not cut-off my descendant's after me, and that you will not destroy my name from my father's house. So David swear to Saul, and he went home, but David and his men went up to the stronghold.

This is a great lesson for us as children of God that in any situation or circumstances, we should allow the will of God to prevail, in doing so. He will surely fight our battles and we shall have our peace.

"Blessed are the merciful, for the shall obtain mercy".Matt.5:7

CHAPTER TWO
THE PRICE OF OBEDIENCE

It was Jesus Himself who said "why do you call me Lord, and do not do the things that I tell you". Living in God's kingdom requires a life of obedience. He has chosen us and He also chooses the way we are to go. Jesus did not choose for Himself. He only did what the Father showed Him to do. He is the pattern Son, and we need to follow His example. We can make choices, and pride ourselves with having made a right choice when all goes well, and blame other when it doesn't.

Most Christians do not recognize that SELF sits on the throne in the Doctrine of "FREE CHOICE". It is the principle doctrine of the kingdom of the knowledge of good and evil, when we insist that we have to choose to obey, the source of that decision is self, and self is still on the throne. Can you picture the state of an army where the general gives a command, and soldiers sit down to discuss the pros and cons of that command? Then after a lengthy debate, they choose whether or not to obey the command. When Christ is Lord in our life He is on the throne. He gives the orders and we follows those order.

This is 'OBEDIENCE'. Jesus learned obedience by the things which he suffered.

"Though he were a son, yetlearned he obedience bythe things which hesuffered". (Heb.5:8) NKJV.

Suffering test of our obedience will we remain forgiving and loving when we are treated with contempt, when we are despitefully used, or when we are tortured mentally or physically for righteous sake. Christ's devotion to obedience was so great and complete that He passes every test with glowing colors. He learned that obedience is costly. He exhibited the humility and faith that was needed to pass every test. It will also cost us our pride, and selfhood, it will cost our money, it will cost our rights, reputations, relationships and everything that is dear to self.

Everything He says is truth, and therefore reliable. He cannot err! If we do not understand His ways, it is because His ways are higher than our ways. We cannot understand His way with our natural thinking, because the spiritual is higher than the natural. Without the knowledge of the very essence of God and His love for us, we will doubt His ability and judgment and wonder if we have the strength to pass the test.

We will view ourselves as grasshoppers in comparison with the giant difficulties confronting us, just like the Israelites did when they saw the giants that occupied the land God had promise them. Their focus shifted from the power of God to their limited ability; they forget that it was God who said that He would give them the land for possession.

We too need to keep our eyes fixed constantly on Jesus the author and finisher of our faith, obedience will cost us everything that is of self, all our rebellion and every thought that is against the rule of Christ.

As a peculiar people an holy Nation, it behold on us to part away with self and enthrone Christ as captain and Lord of our lives.

The book Exodus 19:5 tell us expressly what exactly God requires from the people of Israel which to obey His voice indeed and keep his covenant, he said then they shall be a peculiar treasure into Him above all others people on the earth. Since we're the spiritual Israelites, if we key into this covenant blessing we shall be a peculiar indeed because God is not a respecter of persons.

"Now therefore, if you will indeed obey My voice and keep My covenant, then you shall be a special treasure toMe above all people; for all the earth is Mine". (Exodus 19:5) NKJV.

Therefore Dying to self means - changing your activities, changing your life-style,altering your desire. It meant not reacting with your emotions when people speak badly of you. If something happens and you react emotionally by getting offended or wounded, that shows there is a place in your heart that is not totally yielded. Yielded flesh does not react. Neither lie not. When you lie, you shock the Almighty God. Since you claim to be His son. His Name is the TRUTH. How could the son of the TRUTH lie? Flattery and exaggeration would bring repulsion to the Almighty God. Tell the Truth as it is, and leave it at that.

You must prepare to follow hard after God with determination, and ready to move beyond the level of desire to that of determination. Your desire to do the will of God must be strong that you are prepared to pay the prize. It takes your boldness and determination to get through every barrier placed at every distance on your pathway, refused to be discouraged, because he, (the enemy of your soul) will do all he would to distract your attention with pressure from every side, but be focused and never give up! As an instrument in the porter's hand you must be steadfast and unmovable.

Also learn how to forgive others. It is John Maxwell that says: "People who find it difficult to forgive don't see themselves realistically. They are either terribly arrogant or tremendously insecure". If you don't have peace, it's not because someone took it from you. You gave it away. You cannot always control what happen to you, but you can control what happen in you.

SELF DISCIPLINE:

"Know you not that they whichrun in a race run all, but one receive the prize? So run thatyou may obtain". I cor.9:24.

Dear Reader! Realize this fact that lazy dreamers will never achieve the high goal of spiritual maturity without self-discipline in appetites, emotions, moods, speech and priorities.

The term discipline carries a variety of meanings. To the child, it mean being compelled to do something undesirable and being punished if he rebels. Discipline means compulsion,Pain, authority. To the soldier discipline means conformity to regulations, instance obedience to orders. To students it means the course of instructions he understands with the specific requirements and rules and examination to it. The child, the Soldier, the student, the discipline is all correct. But there is something more. The aim of child discipline, or military or academic or religious, is to discipline character which goes beyond the minimum whole life. Imposed discipline must lead to self-discipline, it is even possible for the Christian to be a sincere and regenerated follower of Jesus yet remain undisciplined in many area of life. One may be purified from the carnal mind and filled with the spirit, yet be merely on the hold of that larger discipline of full maturity. In a general sense,self-discipline is the ability to regulate conduct by principle and judgment rather than impulse, desire, high pressure, or social custom. It is basically the ability to subordinate.

APPETITES:
there are several aspects here for one thing, there is included the ability to subordinate to the body and its physical appetites to the service of the mind. My previous experience will exemplified on how I became convinced that eating of much kolanut was affecting my eyes sight. After visiting a doctor who diagnosed my dizziness to too much of intake of particular fruit. He advised me to reduce the intake of the kolanut drastically so that the dizziness may be cleared. But I decided to stop the eating of kolanut despite I had enjoyed it all along. When it becomes a matter of choice between my sight and kolanut, the lesser value has to give way. Since then, I have never tasted

kolanut neither do I have any problem with my sight as a result of self-discipline.

EMOTIONS:

Emotions must be subordinate to the reason. Too often the mind serves only the purpose of devising excuses for doing what the heart want to do. The heart needs to be first cleansed, and then kept on the leash of discipline. Then it can safely become the co-partner with the mind in living according to fixed principles. The disciplined man has learned this art. He distrusts his sudden impulse.Not that he is cold and calculating, he may be warm and sympathetic, but he has grown up "into Christ" and is not about "tossed to and fro" and carried about either by every wind of doctrine" or the winds of impulse, fancy, and strange feelings.

MOODS:

Disciplined character also means the misery of moods. There is yet another are of conquest in the subordinate of one's emotions. Actually the need here is twofold, first we must cultivate that fixedness of purpose that steadiness of faith, that quite almost re-think performance of duty which gradually chasten our moods, cleansing from them their fierce wildness and bringing them into keep with our total pattern. Then our moods will less radically. The pendulum, even it is still swings will not swing so far.

Secondly, we must learn to transcend the moods which we cannot entirely elude, some ebb and flow of feellng is inevitable. Some slight shifting of interest orattitude is apt to occur in the steadfast personality. A failure in our workcombined with physical weariness may bring a cloud of depression and discouragement. A windy day, a letter from home front, a personal misunderstanding is some of the many little things which play on our spirits and produce some variations on our feelings. Possibly a touch of nostalgia loneliness.

With the changed mood may come strange impulses which we dare not heed - may be to take a trip, or make an unwise purchase, or neglect some duty, impulses willnot pass one's common sense in sober moments. With the changed mood also may come the temptation to let our mood slow. There is danger or appearing suddenly altered in our relationship with the people around us.

According to the mood we may be abnormally happy, and open or moreso (depressed) and closed, generous to the point of profligacy (wastefulness) or prudent to the point of stinginess, one day we may be optimistic, the next day pessimistic. Because our personalities cannot be relied upon for consistency, our friends do not know what to expect next. At first people are puzzled. Then they learn to say "Just one of his moods", with a hint scorn, and they learn to be wary and apprehensive in all relationships with us, for they never quite know what mood they will find us in, or how soon our mood will change. A mature disciplined Christian has learned 'to feel just as good when he feels bad as he does when he feels good'. In the Lord, and in the quiet steady application of his energies to life. Disciplined character never dissipates time and energy by catering to moodiness. "I don't feel like it", may at times express the plain truth, but the habitual use of that phrase is the trait of the weakling, not the strongman. When a college student explained that he had not attended the last class session because he "didn't feel like it", the professor said "Youngman has it ever occurred to you that most of the world's work is done by people who don't feel like it".

SPEECH:

Regardless of how carefully controlled a person is at all other points, none can qualify for the high rating of a truly disciplined character whose tongue is no restrained by the bride of prudence and directed by the reins of love. This is disciplined "if anyone think himself to be religious, and yet does not bride his tongue but deceives his own heart, this man's religious is worthless". (James 1:26). One may have disciplined body, even disciplined emotions, appetites and habits, but a loose tongue betrays a fatal fault in the armor. The character is defective. Some people prides themselves on their frankness "I say what I think", they boast, so owes the fool, according to the Bible.

"A fool has no delight in understanding, but inexpressing his own heart". (Prob.18:2) NKJV.

Frankness is intelligent having tact and discretion. But it becomes a sadistic (cruel or vicious) vile when it is merely the unbridlederupting of opinions without regard to times and place or human feelings.

"There is one who speaks rashly like the thrusis of a sword, but the tongue of the wise brings healings". (Prob.12:18) NKJV.

Often takes a far higher display of discipline to retrain from speaking than it does to speak. Forbearance is a Christian virtue, even as is frankness.

PRORITIES:

Furthermore, a truly disciplined character has the ability to subordinate the lesser to the greater. Here is the problem of priorities probably the most crucial problem of life. On its solution hangs success or failure, improvement or degeneration, and in the larger sense, heaven or hell.

The battle here is not primarily to acquire a clear perception of what is more important, for all Christiansacknowledge that God and church should hold first place in our lives, without hesitation we would concede that heaven is an infinitely richer goal than earthly position that persons come before profits, that the culture (Cultivation or refinement) of the soul and mind is more to be desired than entertainment, that character is of far greater value than pleasure, usefulness is better than idleness, that soul winning is life's crowning achievement, that righteousness is infinitely more satisfying than popularity. When confronted bluntly with those simple alternatives we know instantly which to approve. We would say "Yes, these are the supreme goal". The problem is actually giving first place to these values in practical daily living and that is a problem primarily of character.

This involves ability to reject day by day that great army, its possible activities which clamor, our precious energy but which would hopper the doing of more important things.

ADJUSTMENT TO AUTHORITY:

The final hallmark of the disciplined character is the ability to assimilate imposed discipline with grace and profit. It is by no means easy to subordinate natural initiative and self-assertion to legitimate authority. But it must be done if one expects maximum happiness and usefulness, and if one desires to achieve a mature character. Being a constitutional rebel is no ground for pride. Habitual rebellion is the cut of weakling rather than the strong. It requires neither intelligence nor character to assert loudly, "No one can tell me what to do". But it requires both submitting to the inescapable and necessary constraint of society, and submitting, not grudgingly but graciously with mature understanding and cheerful good-will.

Finally reader, to be an instrument of honor in the hand of God and a peculiar treasure, it is therefore necessary to adhere strictly to the exposition in this chapter. Because the unbroken chain of obedience is the secret for receiving the substance of God's promise. God expects trust and total obedience from his chosen children.

CHAPTER THREE

HUMILITY:

Humility is the noble choice to forgo your status and use your influence for the good of others. It is to hold your power in service of others. The best leaders are marked by humility.Humility is what makes the great, great this is the exemplary life which Christ exhibit to redeem us from sin.

"But God commandeth hislove towards us, in that whilewe were yet sinners Christ died for us." (Roman 5: 8) NKJV

Let examine the five evidence of humility:

1. **Humility is common sense**; it is a reflection of the deep structure of reality. None of us is an expert of everything, what we don't know and can't do far exceeds what we do know and can do.
2. **Humility is beautiful**; It is a simple psychological reality. We are more attracted to the great who know it and want to know us too. Presumption diminishes greatness, humility enhance greatness. Academic research found that a humility

resolution took place in the middle of the first century. Not only because Jesus crucifixion changed the way had people understood greatness and humility.

The cross of Christ was contrary to the understanding of greatness in the ancient world. The thief at left hand side of Jesus on the cross couldn't understand while Christ cannot safe Himself and them also. Early Christian had to deal with the question. Did His crucifixion mean that wasn't as great as they thought? Greatness must consist a willing sacrifice and holding power for the good of others, of course this is what Matthew 20:28 and Phill.2:3-4

"Just as the Son of Man did notcome to be served, but to serveand to give His life a ransom for many".(Matthew 20:28)NKJV.

"Letnothing be done through selfish ambition or conceit, but in lowliness of mind let each esteem others better than himself. Let each of you lookout not only for his own interests, but also for the interests of others. Let thismind be in you which was also in Christ Jesus, who, beingin the form of God, did notconsider it robbery to be equal with God, but made Himself ofno reputation, taking the formof a bondservant, and comingin the likeness of men. And being found in appearance as a man, He humbled Himself and became obedient to thepoint of

death, even the death of the cross".(Phill.2:3-8) NJKV.

3.***Humility is Generative:****It generates new knowledge, new abilities. The logic is easy; the proud person (say at a conference like this) will go away with less than the humble person who is looking to learn. This is even true in science. Think about how science works. It is basically a humble confession that you can't just observe the world and describe it's you have to test your theory.*

4. ***Humility is Persuasive:****The goal a persuasion is to influence others in a way that will produce voluntary change in their attitude and behavior. To produce this kind of voluntary change. You must impact people at the level of belief, because people only become willing to change what they believe. Nothing has a greater impact on what people believe than the perception that they are being told the truth. Therefore the controlling factor in persuasion is Humility.*

5.**Humility is inspiring:**The real power is effective leadership is maximizing other people's potential, which inevitably demands ensuring they get the credit, when our ego wouldn't let us build another person up, then the effectiveness of the organization goes down. When leaders appear aloof and unapproachable, we admire them, but we don't imitate them. But humble leaders, we don't just admire them; we aspire to be like them. Four tests of leadership, ability, authority, character and persuasion. Some of the most inspiring leaders in history had no structural authority. They just had truckloads of ability, character and persuasion. Sometimes, you don't need the power of armies to change emirs or individuals. Humility is the answer.

Therefore in proclaiming the good-news, persuasion and humility is the key factors.

"Go ye therefore, and teach, allnations, baptizing them in thename of the father, and of theSon, and of the Holy Spirit.Teaching them to observe all things whatever. I have commanded you and. Lo I amwith you, always, even to the end of the age. Amen".(Matthew 28:19-20) NKJV.

CHAPTER FOUR

THE REWARD OF OBEDIENCE: God always gives us something better than the things he takes from us. He takes away the worthless to give us the priceless. His rewards are for the overcomers. To be an overcomers we have to learn obedience, for only in obedience can we walk in agreement with God.

We have to believe that God's will for us, because is better than our own will. Only in submission to God can we rule with Him over our own lustful desires. As we feed in Christ, we will learn to be obedient to the Lord whose word is a sword that cut-off all our fleshly desires.

Hearing ears are necessary for learning obedience. These are not physical ears that pick-up physical vibrations, but inside ears that can hear the spirit. Not everyone has them. Jesus said my sheep hear My voice. Only the sheep in the shepherd's flock have spiritual ears. We received them when we were born again. So let's use them, one of the mark of a born again Christian is the ability to hear what the spirit is saying. He always convey true spiritual messages that are customize to fit our need. If we do not hear the spirit, we will hear lies and follow them. It requires humility of heart to hear them; those who are full of pride consider themselves to be self-sufficient and in need of nothing.Hearing implies obedience. Children may hear what their parents have said, but when they do not obey we say that they did not hear them. To hear what the spirit says means we are obedient to His instructions.

Obedience has great rewards, our measure of obedience is revealed in the depth of the difficulties, adversity, and the allurements of the flesh that need to be overcome. Obedience activates our death to Sin, it brings death to our self-will and our selfhood. It is the only way in which we can experience the power of the life we have in Christ and thus grows spiritually.

In the book of Revelation Chapters 2 and 3 we find some of the great rewards are for us while we are still living on planet earth. Look at the wonderful promise in verse 7. "Hewho has an ear, let him hear what the spirit says to the churches. To him who overcomes. I will grant to eat of the tree of life, which is in the Paradise of God". Here is a beautiful promise of blessing limited to overcomers, those who are obedient; we can never be overcomers in disobedience.

Therefore the tree of life is for those who desire to escape tribulation, not for those who depend upon their own ability to make right choices. Overcoming is not always a popular word, because it carries with it the knowledge that there will be testing and trials, obstacles will be placed in one's way, and they have to be overcome by faith in obedience to what the spirit is saying.

Listening to the spirit does away with carnal thinking, for carnal thinking is always against the spirit. We have been called out of carnal thinking into spiritual thinking. God has purposed that His ecclesia (His called out ones) shall receive the mind of Christ to their strength and victory.

Overcomer allow Christ to rule them, they do not obey their carnal thinking. Christ is the Captain of our salvation; He is the first-born, He is the first to triumph over all the lusts of the flesh by His spirit it comes to live in us and rule us until our very thought and action are under His control.

The Christ in us is the power, the dynamo that overcomes every lie, every deception and every hurt at us this is the omnipotence of Christ; in his strength there is power and victory.

To eat of this tree we have to be in paradise, because that is where this tree is found. Paradise is the place where God rules. It is with the kingdom of God. Jesus said that the kingdom of God is with us. God rules us by His spirit who has been poured into our hearts. Therefore only those who have overcomes the enticements of the natural mind are able to follow the spirit's directives and keep Christ's deeds. They do not do their own will, never as Christ did not do his own will.

Those who have learned by obedience will be given authority, for they can be trusted to carry out the Father's wishes. God gives those who hear His voice, and have learned to obey His voice the right to act on His behalf. They are God's Ambassadors.

"As an earring of gold, and an ornament of fine gold,So is a wise reprover uponan obedient ear". (Proverbs 25:12) NKJV.

CONCLUSION

In conclusion, we've been told in this book our responsibility as peculiar treasure unto our God. We must fall in lines to His calling of hearken to His voice and keeping the covenant. This is our primary duty to God, and we cannot avoid to fail Him who has called us out of darkness into His marvelous light to be the brightness of His glory. We should realize this fact that no man is able to accomplish a task successfully unless he seeks God's guidance and obeys same faithfully. We must be obedient to God. He has no time for rebellious, disobedient people. No matter how tasking or difficult the assignment or bidding may seem, we are to be strong, courageous and prayerfully cling to God's hand as we struggle or battle through. We must remember that He who has promises is faithful (Heb.10:23).

The book also admonished the readers to have listening ears, because there is wisdom in listening. Also encourages us how to learn by obedience in the fear of the Lord.

"I know that whatever God does. It shall be forever.Nothing can be added to it.And nothing taken from it,God does it, that men should fear before Him".(Ecclesiastes 3:14) NKJV.

Therefore, if you are born-again child of God, dead to self, sin and pride, obedient with humble spirit, having a listen ears to hear what the spirit says, and adhere strictly to his directives. Assuredly you will eat of the tree of life which is in the midst of paradise and in addition you will become God's Ambassador on earth, then be entrusted to act on behalf of God.

Finally dear readers, let us hear the conclusion of the whole matter. "Fear God, and keep his commandments; For this is the whole duty of man". Eccl.12:13.

Be A Peculiar Treasure unto God - Shalom.

Take note of these words as your reference point:

1. Now therefore, if you will obey my voice, indeed, and keep my covenant, then ye shall be a peculiar treasure unto me above all people for all earth is mine".(Exodus 19:5) NKJV.
2. "Be strong and of good courage, do not fear nor be afraid of them. for the Lord your God. He is the One who goes with you. He will not leave you nor forsake you". (Duet.31:5) NKJV.
3. "for God will bring every work into judgments, Including every secret thing, whether good or evil". (Eccl.12:14) NJKV
4. "God is not man, that He should lie, nor a son of man, that He should repent. Has He said, and will He not make it good";(Number 23:19) NKJV.

5. "You will show me the pathof life; In Your presence in fullness of joy; At your right hand are pleasure forevermore". (Psalm16:11) NJKV.

Let's make this declaration;

1. I CONFESS to God that I am a sinner and belief that the LORD Jesus Christ died for my sins on the cross and was raise for my justification. I do now receive Him as my personal Lord and Saviour.
2. "Stand fast therefore in the liberty by which Christ has made us free, and be not entangled again with a yoke of bondage".(Galatians 5:1) NKJV.

BE A PERCLIAR TREASURE UNTO GOD.

Tel: 0818-868-0576, 0805-712-0673.
E-mail: Emmanuelafolabi2@gmail.com
Emmanuelinterest05@yahoo.com

Postal Address:
No 28 New Jerusalem Street,
Ije-Ododo, Ijegun,
Lagos- state,
Nigeria.
Phone: 0818 868 0576

About the book

In this book. A peculiar treasure readers were made to know that God made man as His last creation in His own image. God loved His creature, man because a lot of things has been bestowed upon man. God tried to replicate Himself on earth, to accomplish this, He breathe his breathe into man, for man to function like Him, God enjoys fellowshipping with man.

To become God's beloved treasure, Christians have to reciprocal God's love in their daily living, love can only develop if the other party plays his part.

The creator of heaven and earth is a principle God, therefore the only thing He requires from man is total obedience. As many that trend on the part of obedience, God draws them nearer to Himself. Thus, they become His peculiar treasure.

In addition, God requires service and true worship from man to create a closer connection between both parties. This book elaborates how one can go about it, to become God's peculiar treasure.

I recommend this piece of work to every Christian and whosoever want to get closer to God, a must read.

I also appreciate the author of this book, Emmanuel O. Afolabi to allow me air my opinion in this book. May God continually bless you with abundant insights of drawing men unto Him and reward your love for His Kingdom's business accordingly.

Deacon Wale Ogunleye
Foursquare Gospel Church in Nigeria
Zion Assembly
Ije-Ododo,
Lagos – Nigeria

AUTHOR BIOGRAPHY

Emmanuel O. Afolabi a season teacher, blogger and author, a product of LIFE Bible College Ikorodu, has held several positions in many branches of Foursquare Gospel Church in Nigeria since his salvation over three decades ago.

He has worked in the Christians Education Department where he was once the Discipleship Superintendent, Assistant General Sunday School Superintendent for many years amongst others. Presently, he is General Sunday School superintendent and Church Secretary of Foursquare Gospel Church, Zion Assembly, Ije-Ododo, Ijegun, Lagos State.

He was formerly Purchasing Manager/Clearing Officer of Fareast Merchandise Coy. Ltd &Panalpina World Transport (Nig) Ltd.

He is married and blessed with God's Treasure to His own glory.

Emmanuel O. Afolabi

Other Books By Emmanuel O. Afolabi

THE BATTLE OF IDENTITY

HOW TO RECOVER FROM PAINFUL LOSSES

THE PATHWAYTOHONOR